What Bluebirds Do

Pamela F. Kirby

BOYDS MILLS PRESS

HONESDALE, PENNSYLVANIA

*Thanks to Kenn Kaufman and Kimberly Kaufman
for their thoughtful comments on this book.*

Credits: All photographs are by Pamela F. Kirby except for pages 3 (courtesy of Elaine Sawyer Whittemore) and 41 (Tom Grey). The quotation of Laurance Sawyer is used by permission of Elaine Sawyer Whittemore.

Boyds Mills Press, Inc.
815 Church Street
Honesdale, Pennsylvania 18431
Printed in China

Library of Congress Cataloging-in-Publication Data

Kirby, Pamela F.
  What bluebirds do / Pamela F. Kirby. — 1st ed.
    p. cm.
  Includes bibliographical references.
  ISBN 978-1-59078-614-7 (hardcover : alk. paper)
  1. Bluebirds—Juvenile literature. I. Title.

  QL696.P288K57 2009
  598.8′42—dc22

                            2008034057

First edition
Designed by Tim Gillner
The text of this book is set in 18-point Optima.

10 9 8 7 6 5 4 3 2 1

Author's Note

My interest in Bluebirds was ignited by Laurance Sawyer of Ringgold, Georgia, in the 1980s. Laurance was the son of the late Edmund Joseph Sawyer, a renowned naturalist and artist. He instilled in Laurance a love of nature and a desire to do his part as a conservationist. Laurance's care for Bluebirds and conservation efforts sparked an interest within me, and I have had Bluebirds in my yard ever since.

That's where I took the images for this book. As I sat in the blind that spring and watched those marvelous Bluebirds raise their families, I wanted to share their wonderful story with young readers. The story happened as it is written. The behaviors and events are actual. The Bluebirds lived the story. I took the images and lots of notes. I hope the birds' beautiful story will ignite the same interest within others that Laurance Sawyer did within me. Maybe, just maybe, it will create a desire in people to take care of Mother Earth.

— *P.F.K.*

For this is home to a loving pair
whose song is one of love;
Whose very life of spreading joy
points us to One above.

—Laurance Sawyer (1910–1994)

Laurance and Adelaide Sawyer

3

This is a story of a pair of Eastern Bluebirds that built a nest in my backyard.

They laid eggs, hatched the eggs, and raised their chicks.

The male Bluebird (dad) is bright blue on
his head, back, wings, and tail, with
a rusty chest and white underbelly.

The female Bluebird (mom) has a pale blue head and back, with lighter blue wings and tail and lighter rusty chest.

Her dull colors help her and the chicks blend with the trees and bushes, where they hide from predators.

Indigo Bunting

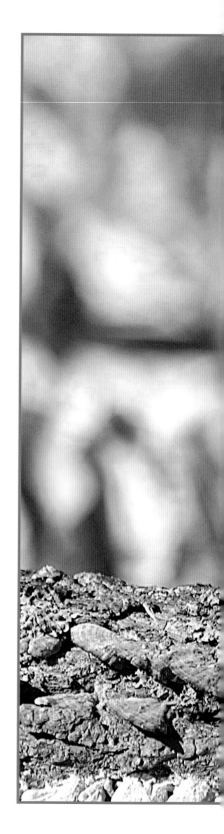

There are other blue birds.

They look different from the Bluebird.

One bird is called the Indigo Bunting.

It has a mixture of blues all over, with black on its wings.

It has a gray beak.

Another blue bird is called a Blue Jay.

It is bigger than the Bluebird, and it has a pointed crest on its head, like a cap, and a different pattern on its body.

Blue Jay

In the springtime, the Bluebirds met.

The male wanted the female to be his mate.

He would wave his wings as he sang to her.

The Bluebird held a worm in his beak and sang at the same time.

The male often gave food to the female as a gift.

The Bluebirds mated, and then they needed
to find a place to build a nest.

Bluebirds are cavity nesters.

They build their nests in closed-in spaces,
such as knotholes, open pipes, or holes
carved out by woodpeckers or other birds.

The male showed the female many nesting places, including the nest box in my backyard.

Notice that he spreads his tail feathers to support his body at the hole.

The female chose my nest box built just for Bluebirds.

Bluebirds usually take ten or eleven days to build the nest.

It's made of loose grasses, pine needles, and twigs.

The female laid five blue eggs, usually one egg each morning over five days.

She sat on the eggs to keep them warm,
taking time out only to stretch or
hunt for food.

Often, the male would bring food to her.

The eggs hatched after eleven days.

Now there were five baby Bluebirds to care for.

The female was young.

She behaved as if this was her first family.

She had trouble staying on the nest.

She would catch food and hold it in her beak while the male fed the babies.

She fed the babies half as much food as the male did.

He showed her what to do, and then

she fed the babies also.

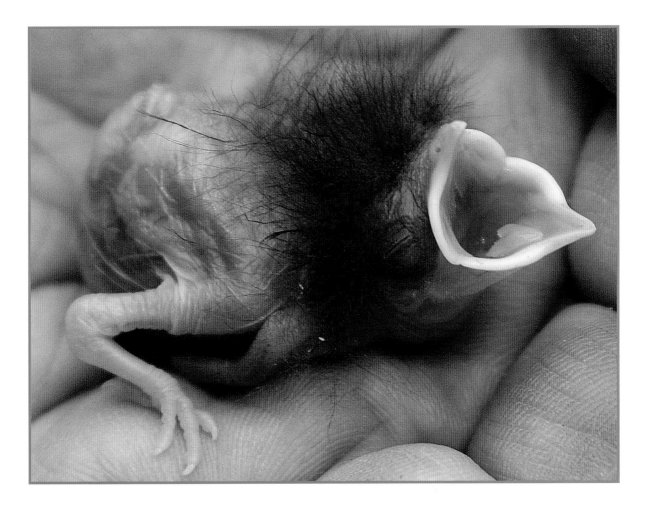

The babies grew big, strong, and healthy.

When they hatched, they were covered in gray down—small, fuzzy feathers that kept them warm.

After twelve days, the down was
replaced by bigger feathers.

Now they had spotted chests and heads,
with blue wings and tails.

There was little room in the nest to
stretch their wings.

They did not have to be taught to fly;
they just knew how by instinct.

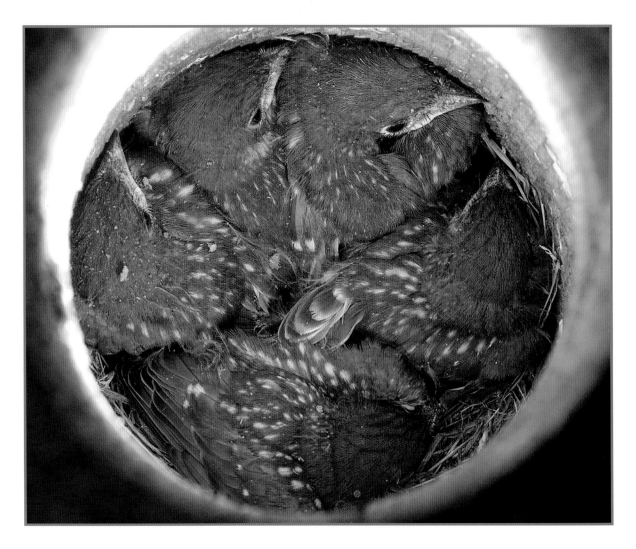

The baby Bluebirds ate mostly insects, worms, and berries.

I put out extra food, such as mealworms and crickets.

Feeding the chicks kept the parents busy.

First, the male gave a worm or insect to the female,

and she fed the babies.

As the chicks grew and wanted more food, both parents fed the chicks.

The parents ate only after the chicks were quiet.

The parents kept the nest clean.

The chicks' droppings came in tiny bags called fecal sacs.

The parents dropped each one far from the nest.

When the babies were fifteen days old,
they wanted food more often.

They took turns sitting in the nest-box hole, watching the world outside.

Can you spot the wasp the chick is watching?

The chicks became more restless and called to their parents.

See the feathers fluffed in his neck?

He can call without opening his beak.

The parents sat in the trees nearby.

They began to lure the chicks from the box by bringing them less food.

The chicks sat in the hole and called for something to eat.

Sometimes they called with their beaks closed.

Sometimes they just begged with their beaks open.

Finally, the chicks left the nest.

One by one, they stood at the edge of the hole and—with a burst of speed—

jumped out of the nest.

They flew to a nearby tree.

A chick's first flight from the nest
is called fledging.

Once that happens, the baby bird
is called a fledgling.

(The difference between the two words
is the second *l* in *fledgling*.)

The fledglings called to their parents.

The parents called back.

They were trying to get all the young ones into the same tree.

The fledglings flew in different directions at first.

Finally, they flew into the same tree.

They followed the parents into the woods.

There they would learn to take care of themselves.

The first week, the fledglings stayed in one area and the parents brought food to them.

The second week, the fledglings
followed their parents around and the
parents fed them.

The third week, the young birds began to search for food in the trees, staying near the parents.

The fourth week, the fledglings began to
fly down to the ground and catch bugs
or worms for food.

The fifth week, the young ones could fly well and feed themselves.

They were pretty much on their own.

They still stayed close together, near their parents.

New feathers kept growing.

By fall, the young birds had rusty-colored chests and blue heads to match their beautiful blue wings and tails.

They had become little Bluebirds.

Three Bluebirds

Three kinds of Bluebirds live in North America: the Eastern Bluebird, the Mountain Bluebird, and the Western Bluebird. These cousins are members of the Thrush family. Like other Thrushes, such as the American Robin, they are songbirds with slender beaks and have feet that are good for perching.

Bluebirds grow to be 6 to 8 inches (16 to 21 centimeters) long and weigh about 1 ounce (30 grams). They eat small invertebrates (such as insects, spiders, worms, and slugs) and small fruits. From bird feeders, they prefer mealworms, bits of dried fruit, suet, or a mixture of peanut butter and cornmeal.

Eastern Bluebird

Scientific Name: *Sialia sialis*
Pronunciation: sy-AY-lee-uh SY-uh-liss
Meaning of Name: "a kind of bird"
Summer Range: eastern and central North America from southern Canada south to Mexico and Central America
Winter Range: same as summer range, except for Canada and the northernmost states

Mountain Bluebird

Scientific Name: *Sialia currucoides*
Pronunciation: sy-AY-lee-uh kur-you-KOY-dees
Meaning of name: "bird that looks like a warbler"
Summer Range: throughout much of western North America, western Canada, and central Alaska
Winter Range: Oregon and south through the Southwest and into central Mexico

Western Bluebird

Scientific Name: *Sialia mexicana*
Pronunciation: sy-AY-lee-uh MEKS-ih-KAY-nah
Meaning of Name: "bird of Mexico"
Summer Range: southwestern Canada, Pacific Northwest, and much of the Southwest
Winter Range: Pacific Coast, the Southwest, and south into central Mexico

Bluebirds Through the Year

This book shows an exciting chapter in the lives of Eastern Bluebirds. Sights like these can be seen every summer.

Bluebirds must be at least one year old before they can choose a mate and make a nest. After a pair of adults raises its first family, the birds may nest again. They may have two to three families, or broods, a season.

Amazingly, in about three months' time, the Bluebirds meet, nest, and teach their babies to care for themselves. Here are four chicks that are just hatching. One is lying on another chick, which is coming out of its shell. See the tiny wing on the shell? Can you see four chicks?

As cold weather moves in, Bluebirds may fly south. They go where food is available. In places with warmer climates and plenty of food, they may stay. If they do not migrate, they may join more Bluebird families, as well as other northern birds passing through, and form a flock. On cold nights or freezing days, they may gather in a roost cavity to stay warm.

For Bluebirds that do not migrate, food can be scarce in freezing weather. Some kinds of plants have berries into winter, which the birds may eat. This season is a good time for people to provide Bluebirds with extra food, such as suet, mealworms, raisins, currants, and dried fruit. Bluebirds swallow their food whole, so make the portions small.

A Chipping Sparrow knocks a female Bluebird off the nest box.

Bringing Back the Bluebirds

Bluebirds were once in danger of disappearing. Their numbers began to decrease with the introduction of birds from other countries, especially the House Sparrow (also called the English Sparrow) in 1851 and the European Starling in 1890. These birds spread rapidly.

House Sparrows are aggressive and try to destroy the Bluebird's nest and eggs. They can even kill the chicks or the parents.

The Starling is bigger and will steal the nest and eat all the berries in the nesting area.

As people built more houses and other buildings, orchards and tree holes near fields began to disappear. With fewer places to live, Bluebirds continued to decline. Farmers used pesticides on their crops to kill insects, but the Bluebirds ate the insects and sometimes they died as a result.

With the number of Bluebirds decreasing, concerned people took action. In 1978, with the help of the North American Bluebird Society and its founder, Dr. Lawrence Zeleny, people began to set up and monitor Bluebird nest boxes all across the continent. (A group of nesting boxes that is set up in a habitat suitable for Bluebirds is called a Bluebird trail.)

People all over North America are still working to help the Bluebirds by setting up Bluebird trails in their areas, designing nest boxes that Starlings and House Sparrows will not use, and discouraging insects from invading the nests.

Because of the hard work of these bird lovers, the number of Bluebirds has increased over the years.

Bluebirds in Your Yard

More nesting boxes are needed today. This is where you can help. You can enjoy having Bluebirds in your yard also.

Through the North American Bluebird Society, your library, a bookstore, or the Internet, you can learn how to attract Bluebirds and other wildlife to your yard.

In many areas you may find a local Bluebird Society and places that anyone can visit to see where Bluebirds nest.

Remember, these birds are wild, and as much as we would like to pet them, we should leave them alone. It's okay to look, but do not touch. If you find an injured bird, contact a wildlife rehabilitation expert and ask what you can do to help.

Nature has so much for us to see and appreciate. It is our privilege to protect wildlife. In return, we can have many joyful moments watching them live around us.

Acknowledgments

I would like to thank many others for encouraging me to write this book. First, to the Creator for giving such beautiful and entertaining Bluebirds, and to the Bluebirds for accepting my presence during such a personal time.

Many thanks to mentors and dear friends such as Helen Longest-Saccone and Marty Saccone, Charles Bush, Bill Kenny, Bill Liszka, and Bob Bedwell for their feedback, expertise, and encouragement.

My thanks go to my sister, Jo, for her knowledge of how to command the English language to capture a child's interest and for her belief in me.

Many thanks to Cindy Waisner for her patient proofreading and care for relating this story to young people.

To my mother, who encouraged my love for nature and the joy one can receive just by being outdoors.

And I must thank my technical advisers—Will Zimmerman, Glenn Zimmerman III, and Grasyn Waisner—for their expertise as young readers and nature lovers.

Thanks to my family—Cierra, Mike, Laura, Payton, Lula, Charlie, Deb, Jimmy, Faith and Terry, Glenn and Molly, Phil and Charlene, Don and Shellie, Tom and Donna, Bill, Linda R., George, Jason, and the PowerHouse Kids—for their love and encouragement.

Most of all, thanks to my champion husband, Darrell, whose strength has carried me, encouraged me, and supported my love for photography and my dream of leaving a beautiful story for children.

And, of course, there is Chico, our dog, who waited patiently while I was making images in the blind.

For More Information

Books

Berger, Cynthia, Keith Kridler, and Jack Griggs. *The Bluebird Monitor's Guide.* New York: HarperResource, 2001.

Cruickshank, Allan D., and Helen G. Cruickshank. *1001 Questions Answered About Birds.* New York: Dover Publications, 1976.

Davis, Wayne H., and Philippe Roca. *Bluebirds and Their Survival.* Lexington: University Press of Kentucky, 1995.

Harrison, Hal H. *Eastern Birds' Nests.* Peterson Field Guides. New York: Houghton Mifflin, 1975.

Heilman, Joan Rattner. *Bluebird Rescue.* Country Life Nature Guide. Charlotte, VT: Camden House, 1992.

Kaufman, Kenn. *Lives of North American Birds.* Boston: Houghton Mifflin, 1996.

McKinley, Michael D. *How to Attract Birds.* Des Moines: Ortho Books, 1995.

Pearman, Myrna, and Pauline Mosseau. *Children's Bluebird Activity Book.* Ronan, MT: Mountain Bluebird Trails, 2007.

Ritchison, Gary. *Eastern Bluebird.* Wild Bird Guides. Mechanicsburg, PA: Stackpole Books, 2000.

Sawyer, E. J. *The Best Bird Houses: How to Make Them.* Seattle, WA: Cone Mail Advertising, 1955.

Sibley, David Allen. *The Sibley Guide to Birds.* New York: Alfred A. Knopf, 2000.

Stokes, Donald, and Lillian Stokes. *The Bluebird Book: The Complete Guide to Attracting Bluebirds.* Boston: Little, Brown, 1991.

Stokes, Donald, and Lillian Stokes. *A Guide to Bird Behavior*. Stokes Nature Guides. Boston: Little, Brown, 1989.

Tekiela, Stan. *Birds of the Carolinas Field Guide*. 2nd ed. Cambridge, MN: Adventure Publications, 2004.

Thompson, Bill, III. *An Identification Guide to Common Backyard Birds*. Marietta, OH: Bird Watcher's Digest, 1995.

Toops, Connie. *Bluebirds Forever*. Stillwater, MN: Voyageur Press, 1994.

Zickefoose, Julie. *Enjoying Bluebirds More*. Marietta, OH: Pardson, 1993.

Web Sites*

Birding and Wild Birds
www.birding.about.com/Wild Birds

Cornell Lab of Ornithology
www.birds.cornell.edu/AllAboutBirds/BirdGuide/Eastern_Bluebird.html

Eastern Bluebird Rescue Group
www.easternbluebirdrescuegroup.org/index.htm

Laurance Sawyer's Bluebird Housing
www.bluebirdhousing.com
Offers ready-made Bluebird nest boxes.

National Wildlife Federation
www.nwf.org

The Nature Conservancy
www.nature.org

North American Bluebird Society
www.nabluebirdsociety.org
Offers ready-made and build-it-yourself Bluebird nest boxes.

North Carolina Bluebird Society
www.ncbluebird.com

Live Mealworms

The following companies sell one of Bluebirds' favorite foods—mealworms.

Sunshine Mealworms
www.sunshinemealworms.com

Nature's Way
www.thenaturesway.com

Grubco
www.grubco.com

*Active at time of publication

Glossary

Bluebird trail a group of nesting boxes set up in a habitat that is suitable for Bluebirds

Blue Jay a noisy, crested, blue bird, bigger than a Bluebird

brood a family of chicks, usually four to five for Bluebirds

cavity nester a bird that nests in an enclosed space, such as a hole in a tree or a nest box

down a coat of fine, hairlike feathers on a newly hatched chick

Eastern Bluebird a bright blue bird with a rust-colored throat and breast

fecal sac (FEE-kul sak) a packet of body waste, produced by Bluebird chicks while still in the nest, that adult parent birds can dispose of

fledge (flej) to fly for the first time

fledgling (FLEJ-ling) a chick that is learning to fly

habitat (HAB-ih-tat) an area that offers the food, water, shelter, and weather conditions needed by an animal species

instinct a natural behavior that wild animals are born with

Mountain Bluebird a turquoise-blue bird without the rusty colors of the Eastern Bluebird or Western Bluebird

predator (PREH-dah-tur) an animal that hunts other animals for food

prey (pray) an animal that is hunted by other animals for food

roost a place where birds perch or sleep

Western Bluebird a bright blue bird with blue throat, rust-colored breast, and (usually) rust-colored back

wildlife rehabilitator a person who is trained and licensed to give treatment and care to injured wildlife

wing wave the movement of a Bluebird's wings to attract its mate's attention

Bluebirds Rock!

Next time you see a Bluebird, think about how much happiness they give us as we watch them raise their families.